Empowered Schools, Empowered Students

CORWIN CONNECTED EDUCATORS SERIES

Teaching the iStudent: A Quick Guide to Using Mobile Devices and Social Media in the K–12 Classroom
By Mark Barnes @markbarnes19

Connected Leadership: It's Just a Click Away
By Spike Cook @DrSpikeCook

All Hands on Deck: Tools for Connecting Educators, Parents, and Communities
By Brad Currie @bradmcurrie

Missing Voices of EdTech Conversations
By Rafranz Davis @RafranzDavis

Flipping Leadership Doesn't Mean Reinventing the Wheel
By Peter M. DeWitt @PeterMDeWitt

The Edcamp Model: Powering Up Professional Learning
By the Edcamp Foundation @EdcampUSA

Empowered Schools, Empowered Students: Creating Connected and Invested Learners
By Pernille Ripp @Pernilleripp

The Power of Branding: Telling Your School's Story
By Tony Sinanis @TonySinanis and Joseph Sanfelippo @Joesanfelippofc

The Relevant Educator: How Connectedness Empowers Learning
By Tom Whitby @tomwhitby and Steven W. Anderson @web20classroom

Empowered Schools, Empowered Students

Creating Connected and Invested Learners

Pernille Ripp
@pernilleripp

CORWIN
A SAGE Company

FOR INFORMATION:

Corwin

A SAGE Company

2455 Teller Road

Thousand Oaks, California 91320

(800) 233-9936

www.corwin.com

SAGE Publications Ltd.

1 Oliver's Yard

55 City Road

London EC1Y 1SP

United Kingdom

SAGE Publications India Pvt. Ltd.

B 1/I 1 Mohan Cooperative Industrial Area

Mathura Road, New Delhi 110 044

India

SAGE Publications Asia-Pacific Pte. Ltd.

3 Church Street

#10-04 Samsung Hub

Singapore 049483

Copyright © 2015 by Corwin

Printed in the United States of America

A catalog record of this book is available from the Library of Congress.

ISBN 978-1-4833-7183-2

This book is printed on acid-free paper.

Executive Editor: Arnis Burvikovs

Associate Editor: Ariel Price

Editorial Assistant: Andrew Olson

Production Editor: Amy Schroller

Copy Editor: Janet Ford

Typesetter: C&M Digitals (P) Ltd.

Proofreader: Dennis W. Webb

Cover and Interior Designer: Janet Kiesel

Marketing Manager: Lisa Lysne

Certified Chain of Custody

SUSTAINABLE FORESTRY INITIATIVE

Promoting Sustainable Forestry

www.sfiprogram.org

SFI-01268

SFI label applies to text stock

14 15 16 17 18 10 9 8 7 6 5 4 3 2 1

Contents

Preface   vii

    Peter M. DeWitt

Acknowledgments   ix

About the Author   xi

Introduction   1

PART 1. THE NEED TO EMPOWER OUR SCHOOLS   3

    Leadership Refelection   4

    Declaration of Intent   4

    Plan of Action   5

    Implementation   6

1. The Empowered Principal as Role Model   8

    Obstacles   9

    Benefits of Change   11

    Plan of Action   11

2. Revitalizing the Staff Meeting   17

    Obstacles   18

    Benefits of Change   18

    Plan of Action   18

3. Cultivating the Expert Within   21

    Obstacles   22

    Benefits of Change   23

    Plan of Action   23

4. Small Moment Professional Development 29

    Obstacles 30

    Benefits of Change 31

    Plan of Action 31

PART 2. THE NEED TO EMPOWER
    OUR TEACHERS AND OUR STUDENTS 37

    Teaching Style Reflection 38

    Declaration of Intent 38

    Plan of Action 39

    Implementation 41

5. The Empowered Classroom 42

    Obstacles 44

    Benefits of Change 46

    Plan of Action 47

6. Classroom Setup to Signal Change 50

    Obstacles 52

    Benefits of Change 53

    Plan of Action 54

7. Empowered Self—Empowered Learning 56

    Obstacles 59

    Benefits of Change 60

    Plan of Action 60

Conclusion 63

Preface

Welcome to the Connected Educators Series.

The past few years have provided momentous changes for educators: Whether it's the implementation of the Common Core State Standards, educational innovations due to technology, teacher and administrator evaluations, or budget cuts, what is clear is that educational reforms come in different shapes and sizes. For many connected educators, one of the invaluable group support systems essential during these times is the professional learning network, also known as our PLN.

Our PLN can provide innovative ideas, current resources, and sound educational practices that stretch our thinking in ways we haven't yet experienced. Equally as important as how a PLN can professionally expand our horizons, it introduces new friends that we look forward to meeting in person. This Connected Educators Series brings together some important members of my PLN. These are educators with a depth of knowledge and level of experience that help me stay current and up-to-date with my educational practices.

In this series, my book, *Flipping Leadership Doesn't Mean Reinventing the Wheel*, takes the innovative idea of flipping classrooms and presents it at the school leader level, engaging the school community in new and innovative ways. In *Connected Leadership*, Spike Cook shares his experiences moving from a novice to digital leadership and illustrates how other educators can do the same.

Digital experts Tom Whitby and Steven Anderson help increase your digital experience by using Twitter to locate a PLN to engage in daily professional development. In *The Relevant Educator,* Tom and Steve provide a plethora of tools to use and define each and every one. Using those same tools, in their book *The Power of Branding,* Tony Sinanis and Joe Sanfelippo help you to brand your school in order to create a positive focus on the learning happening within the four walls. In his book, *All Hands on Deck,* Brad Currie offers us ways to engage with families and students using old techniques with new innovative approaches.

In *Teaching the iStudent,* Mark Barnes provides insight into the life and mind of the iStudent, and in *Empowered Schools, Empowered Students,* Pernille Ripp focuses on empowering students and teachers. Also in the series, in *Missing Voices of EdTech Conversations,* Rafranz Davis shows how equity and diversity are vital to the social media movement and why they are so important to education as we move forward.

Kristen Swanson from the Edcamp Foundation not only focuses on why the Edcamp model is a new innovative way to provide excellent professional development, but she also explains how you can create an Edcamp in your school district in *The Edcamp Model: Powering Up Professional Learning.*

The books in the Connected Educators Series are designed to read in any order, and each provides information on the tools that will keep us current in the digital age. We also look forward to continuing the series with more books from experts on connectedness.

As Michael Fullan has said for many years, technology is not the right driver, good pedagogy is. The books in this connected series focus on practices that lead to good pedagogy in our digital age. To assist readers in their connected experience, we created the Corwin Connected Educators companion website (www.corwin.com/connectededucators) where readers can connect with the authors and find resources to help further their experience. It is our hope and intent to meet you where you are in your digital journey and elevate you as educators to the next level.

Peter M. DeWitt, Ed.D. @PeterMDeWitt

Acknowledgments

Anyone who knows me, knows that I am obsessed with making schools better. My husband, therefore, deserves the most gratitude for the incessant nights discussing education, for always pushing my thinking further, and for reminding me what is most important: the children.

He is not the only person who deserves a thank you. To all of my global colleagues who never falter in their passion, creativity, and dedication—thank you for letting me be a part of something bigger, for letting me be a part of the movement to make education meaningful for everyone, and for giving me so many incredible ideas.

To Peter, Ariel, and Arnis and everyone else at Corwin. I don't know how I got lucky enough to be given this platform to spread a message of empowerment, thank you for seeing something in me that I didn't.

Finally, to the staff at Meriter NICU, who watched me write this book next to the isolette while they so lovingly cared for our premature daughter so that she could come home with us one day. Your love and care shone through in everything you did for Augustine, giving me the peace of mind to try to change the world, one school at a time. My family and I will always be grateful.

About the Author

 Mass consumer of incredible books, **Pernille Ripp** helps students discover their superpowers as a former elementary, but now middle school teacher in Oregon, Wisconsin. She loves children so much that she decided to have four of her own with her soul mate Brandon, who keeps her laughing. She is also the creator of Global Read Aloud (www.globalreadaloud.com), a literacy initiative that since 2010 has connected more than 200,000 students through the use of technology. Her first book was published this May by Powerful Learning Press titled *Passionate Learners—Giving Our Classrooms Back to Our Students*. She muses on education on her blog *Blogging through the Fourth Dimension,* and her work has been featured by *Edutopia, School Library Journal, MiddleWeb,* and *Learning & Leading* magazine as well as in many podcasts and interviews. She teaches others how to give the classroom back to students through webinars, as well as by example, which can be observed by anyone who walks into her classroom.

*To all those children who trusted me with their dreams, empowering me
to try to change the way we teach. But most of all to the children
I have in my arms every day: Theadora, Ida, Oskar, and Augustine—
you are the reason that changing education matters.*

Introduction

Often you can hear my class long before you enter our classroom. Not because the students are out of control, but instead because they are excited. They are out of their chairs, sometimes standing on them instead, using hand gestures and louder voices discussing or figuring out whatever task they have in front of them. Other times, you wouldn't know there are 27 students in our room, because they are all engaged in a quiet discovery that is happening right then. But, regardless of the day what you will find if you walk into my room is a class that is engaged, a class that has a voice, and a class that is globally connected. My class wasn't always like this; this was not how I started out teaching. I realized that if I wanted a classroom filled with joy, with students who actually wanted to be there, then I could not teach as if I were the only one that mattered, as if my words were the only ones that held power. So, I shifted control back to my students, empowering them to become independent learners and problem solvers, giving them a voice to the world so that they can truly discover their place in it.

I wrote this book hoping to inspire others to shift the power held within their schools and classrooms—to start a discussion on who has the power within our school and what does that power structure mean for the entire community of learners. This book is therefore intended to be a practical how-to guide to empower staff and students, to create a community where everyone has a voice, but also a place to use that voice for the betterment of all. This book is designed for anyone involved in education to pick up, find a few ideas, and be inspired to change. I guarantee it is worth your time.

PART 1

The Need to Empower Our Schools

I remember the first time I was called to the principal's office as an adult. The sweaty palms, my mind racing with questions, my heart in my throat. Questions about what I had done to spark a one-on-one meeting taunted me the whole way there, and it wasn't until I sat down in the chair and my principal smiled at me that I actually took a breath. I don't remember now what the conversation was about, probably something about my students, but the experience of being called into an unannounced meeting, of entering into someone else's territory left a deep impression; it left me feeling powerless as I walked into a situation I knew nothing about. It also prompted me to think of what I did to my students whenever I held them back from recess silently admonishing them to stay behind, or asked to speak with them outside of my classroom. How they must have felt their adrenaline spike; how they must have wondered what they had done wrong.

That feeling of powerlessness and that fear of what's to come is a feeling I don't want to give to children or school staff unless it is warranted. Yet, most of our schools are set up with a very clear hierarchy of power. The principal or lead administrator holds most of the control and delegates morsels of it to chosen people, much like in our classrooms where the teacher holds the rein of power and only briefly lets students take control. This type of structure works by feeding itself—all important decisions are made by those in power and one must be given power to have any importance. It is a structure that has not been questioned for a long time, but I feel it is time. It is time to spread the control, to give schools back to the staff, to give classrooms back to the students, and to empower others.

The empowered school is one where all voices are heard, dissenting opinions are valued, and staff is trusted. The principal is not simply the leader, but a voice in the discussion—just not *THE* voice. Empowered teachers feel they have control over their work environment, that their voice is heard, and that their experience matters. Empowered students know that their opinion matters, that they have control over their learning journey, and that school is worth their time. All of this leads to an environment based on community and trust, where everyone knows they matter. Sound utopian? Perhaps, but it is not. The steps toward a better functioning school are easily started and integrated.

LEADERSHIP REFLECTION

Empowered principals know that to be a true learner, self-reflection is key. After all, one cannot exorcize demons from an environment without knowing first which demons are caused by one's own mind-set or actions. Consequently, questions to ask as you begin this journey to empowerment include:

- Do I feel my staff trust me?
- What stakeholders do I involve in major decisions?
- What is my role in staff collaboration?
- How do I feel about change?

To help with this process, there is a more thorough leadership reflection form posted on our companion website.

DECLARATION OF INTENT

The principal has the opportunity to really come through as a leader when declaring the intent to institute a change in the school. It is powerful to discuss one's personal journey of change, and if done well, it can set the tone for the rest of staff to embrace the notion of change in their classrooms. It is vital for the staff to know the *why* behind your desire to change, so have an explanation ready—and expect questions: Why is this change necessary? Why is it urgent? Why should staff care? Allow time to question, to discuss, and to invite teachers to start their own self-reflection that can be done individually or in groups (see Part 2). Who is brave enough to share what they need to change within their own classrooms? Assure everyone that this is not just another staff meeting, but rather the start of a journey. Even look at the setup of your meeting: Are all the chairs facing you, or is the arrangement more conducive for a discussion group? Change starts right at this meeting, so the meeting room should signal that. The next chapter discusses how to create a collaborative staff meeting as part of that change.

PLAN OF ACTION

Once the declaration has been made and discussed, it is time to develop a plan of action. You should now have your own personal plan of action, but it is vital for you and all the other staff to develop one for the school.

While you may have your own ideas for how to start the discussion, here are some ideas for you to borrow if you would like to initiate discussions about defining a plan. Ask your staff:

- What does the word *empowered* mean to you?
- What does an empowered teacher look like?
- What does an empowered student look like?
- What is the one thing that this school must change?
- What is the one thing that this principal must change?
- What is the one thing you hope to gain from this change?

Also, plans of action need to be simple. A plan of action should encompass three things: the why (does not need to be written down), the how, and the when. A great place to start is with no more than five goals and make them specific and attainable. More goals can be added as success is achieved.

Some examples of goals are

- we will use inside experts first to move us forward;
- all voices will be heard and given equal weight when discussing initiatives;
- new initiatives can be proposed by anyone;
- staff members will be trusted to collaborate without agendas or supervision on a regular basis;
- responsibility will be shared and everyone will be expected to step into leadership positions;
- staff meetings will no longer be sit-and-get, but rather professional development opportunities; and
- teachers will be trusted to create their own professional development.

This is really the chance for staff to start to discuss what an empowered school means to them and what it should look like in their school. Because all schools, even within the same district, have their own areas for improvement, it is important that the goals chosen are specific to your school. What are the biggest things that need to be changed and how can they be changed? This should not be a principal-led discussion, but it can be facilitated as one.

IMPLEMENTATION

The ease of this transition is vital. Education as a whole is under immense time pressures, and new initiatives are being forced on us from all angles. This empowerment plan of action cannot be seen as forced or as extra work or it will fail. Therefore, the plan should be determined by all of the stakeholders. By the time the discussion is over, everyone should have an assigned or hopefully chosen area of responsibility, including the principal. This is the time to discuss what this transformation looks like in your environment. Specifically, if inside experts are used in staff training, then who are these experts, what will they teach, and when will they teach it? If one of the goals is to shift staff meetings from a sit-and-get experience to one that revolves around learning, then what does that look like, what are the expectations, and who is in charge? The actual plan of implementation cannot be determined until the goals are established.

The Empowered Principal as Role Model

H e fancies himself the *Lone Ranger*. Striding into trouble whenever the call comes into the office that help is needed with a student. He prides himself on his singular way of handling any child, any adult, and any situation that needs discipline. In fact, he often feels like the only sheriff in town. Being a principal can do that to you. Sometimes you think you are the only line of defense, the one that has to solve everything, no matter the time, no matter the case. And you better be able to solve it by yourself because, after all, that's why they pay you the big bucks. But, for the *Lone Ranger* it isn't just a matter of job duty, it is a matter of responsibility. If he can't solve it then no one can—except, that is far from the truth. He is surrounded by many capable adults that want to help him solve the issues. That want to take on the responsibility, but not at this school; this school only has room for one head honcho, and no one ever forgets that.

The *Lone Ranger* principal is not a new phenomenon, nor is it an isolated one. For too many years, principals have functioned alone at the top, thinking that they are the only ones with the right solution, the right fix, or even the ability to make the right decision. But, now with the advent of social media spurring on global education conversations, teachers are clamoring to assume part of the responsibility of running a school. Teachers are stepping up to take on leadership roles, to build better teams and better environments. Teachers are asking to be empowered to make a change, but not all principals are listening. So, why not? What is it that holds administration back from empowering their own staff members?

OBSTACLES

Fear

First, let's start with fear or perhaps insecurity—often these emotions evidence as huge boulders in the field of education. We often fear what we do not know, and that certainly applies when it comes to principals changing the way responsibility is delegated within their buildings. Often, a hierarchy is established and modeled by the district itself and any new principal quickly discovers that this hierarchy is supposed to be promoted and protected. The fear of standing out or shaking things up too soon also holds back many new principals from changing the power structure of a school. But, what about veteran principals? What holds them back from developing a shared responsibility, a culture of empowerment within their school? Fear certainly plays a role here as well, but transforms into fear of the unknown rather than fear of standing out. Many veteran principals also have a tried and true way of running a school that is not broken, so the need for change is not as apparent. Fear or even insecurity can defeat even the greatest of ideas; thus, the first step on the road to empowerment is always facing one's fears, realizing what they are, and then battling them head on.

Lack of Trust

Trust is another major component of the inability to change. Trust can appear abundant at a school on a general level, but below the surface, trust is often only given to a select few staff members and is elusive to earn. Often, principals feel the pressure to make a decision without input from others, or they have a hard time allowing others into their decision-making process, afraid to appear as a weak leader, or they don't want to burden others with what they see as their responsibility. Trust also plays out in whether or not principals believe that teachers will do the right thing. Often assumptions from the past are at play here, coupled with the tendency in education to assume the worst rather than the best. We simply do not trust that others have the same motivation or desire that we do, even if they proclaim otherwise.

Habit

Generally, either through the construction of teams or by similar personalities coming together, schools tend to work in groups. People tend to stay within their same circles because they are easy and familiar. Principals are no different; they often surround themselves with an inner circle of trusted advisors and/or friends who are consulted when decisions need to be made or new initiatives need to be implemented. Whether intentional or not, the creation of an inner circle produces a new hierarchy at a school—a hierarchy known to all, but confronted by few. That inner circle can consist of people in automatic leadership roles, such as specialists or coordinators at the elementary level, through various other administrative posts in middle and high school. Often the inner circle becomes the go-to group for any new ideas, and new people are hardly ever included in this circle. While some principals seem intent on creating this hierarchy, others end up doing it unintentionally simply by reaching out to those who show an interest, and then after a while forgetting to expand their circle. After all, we are habitual creatures; if one person refuses to take on responsibility in the past, then we often assume that he or she will refuse in the future as well. Eventually, why even bother asking?

Time

Time is a major obstacle facing any new initiative in an educational setting. Schools are constantly being told to do more with less, and thus new initiatives are often only embraced if they promise to give us more time or save us more time. Principals are prisoners of time, trying to juggle hundreds of responsibilities all within the constraints of the school day. No wonder many educators assume that it is simply easier to not change anything because it will take up valuable time.

BENEFITS OF CHANGE

The *Empowered Principal* knows that true urgency to change only comes from a fully invested staff:

- Shared responsibility promotes greater trust
- Greater trust leads to a more positive school environment
- Change takes time, but often saves time
- Staff needs to feel valued and valuable for a sense of responsibility

PLAN OF ACTION

Empowering your staff entails several things: it means trusting them to make key decisions that affect more than just their classroom. It means giving them time to work together in teams. It means creating an environment where all voices are heard and even dissenting opinions are thoroughly discussed and evaluated. It means shifting the sense of responsibility away from a single-person system that is focused on the principal to encompassing all staff in a building. And it means building a community of trust that includes all who work in the school, naturally assuming that all stakeholders will do what is best for the children. So, how is this done in today's time-crunched school environment?

1. Complete the reflection leadership form located on the companion website. Remember that to truly change, we have to face what *we* bring into the equation. This reflection also helps you to decide where you can easily change and what to change first.

2. Declare your intentions. This declaration may seem superfluous or even silly, but often teachers feel disenfranchised because they do not know or understand where an initiative is heading. Consequently, if a principal is about to embark on a journey of change that affects everyone at a school, then proper notification should be given.

3. Develop a plan of action. Know that part of empowering your staff means that you do not have to have it all figured out! The plan of action should be developed with your staff setting common goals and deciding which areas to change first.

4. Implement one step at a time. While we often find many areas we want to change, to ensure better staff cooperation it is important to start small and stay focused. Implement at a balanced pace, do it well, and see the trust of your staff grow. If this change is rushed, more disenchantment with the system occurs than is necessary.

5. Get connected! Whether you expand your local circle of educators or you take the plunge into *Twitter* or *Google Plus* to link with a global education community, now is a great time to get connected. Many leaders have initiated significant changes with the support of a worldwide community. This is not the time to feel alone as you try to overhaul your community of learners, and with so many educators willing to share through social media, there is no reason for you to be alone.

Tony Sinanis, an award-winning principal at Cantiague Elementary in New York, embodies what it means to be a connected principal. Although being connected for him only happened a few years ago, his reasoning for why all principals should be connected is powerful.

It was late January and I was finally catching up on some professional reading when I came across an issue of *Scholastic Administrator* magazine. I was immediately intrigued by the cover that featured a man holding a phone in front of his face and the *Twitter* "mascot" sitting atop the phone (I know many of you know the image I'm describing). I had heard a lot about *Twitter,* but was extremely resistant to try it because I always associated it with celebrities (the Kanye Wests and Britney Spears of the world) sharing random thoughts and details about their lives that I had no interest in reading. There was also some talk about using *Twitter* in our district a couple of years ago to communicate with parents, but once again I was resistant—mainly because I didn't know much about the tool. But, here was this guy, a fellow principal in New Jersey, on the cover of the magazine spotlighting how he used *Twitter* to enhance his craft. As I am always looking for ways to make myself a better instructional leader, educator, and colleague, I dove into the article and soon found myself hooked and ready to create my own *Twitter* account!

The guy on the cover turned out to be Eric Sheninger, (@NMHS_Principal), and he was using *Twitter* for the purposes of professional development and for connecting with other like-minded educators. As the Lead Learner of an elementary school, with no other administrator in the building, the leadership experience often leaves me feeling like I'm on my own little island—Isolation Island to be exact. Don't get me wrong, there is rarely a minute when

(Continued)

(Continued)

I am actually alone while at school, but the ability to dialogue, problem solve, or collaborate with other administrators doesn't occur on a regular basis (even though I work
with many dedicated educators). There is something so
exciting and inspiring that happens when dialoguing with
other instructional leaders and administrators about their
experiences, successes, failures, and passions. Although I
have attended conferences in the past, the experiences
didn't necessarily have a lasting impact on my professional
development because the ability to brainstorm, expand,
and collaborate with others on next steps was still that
missing link.

Well, I am happy to share that *Twitter* has changed all
of that for me—BIG TIME! Since joining *Twitter* and learning
the ropes I feel like I jumped off of Isolation Island and made
my way to the Island of Instructional Leaders (and Pioneers)!
Here are just a few things that have happened for me since
joining *Twitter:*

1. I developed an amazing PLN (Personal/Professional
   Learning Network) filled with other passionate and
   knowledgeable educators who challenge me to think
   and push myself to new levels and in directions I never
   imagined!

2. I follow some of the people in education who I respect
   and admire—and not only do I get to read what
   they're thinking about or working on, but I can reach
   out to them directly with a question or comment and
   can usually get a response!

3. I learned the power of the hashtag (#) and how
   using the right tag unlocks a whole other world of
   professional conversations and sharing of ideas!
   Whether it's the #ptchat on Wednesday evenings

or the #edchat on Tuesdays, there are literally hundreds of people online sharing ideas about a specific question, topic, or book, and the flow of ideas is unreal!

4. I learned about *Zite*, which changed the way I start my day. I cannot begin getting ready for the day, if I don't spend time reading through the blogs, posts, and articles organized just for me by *Zite*.

5. I learned about *Google Docs* (and many other *Google* components) that show me different ways to harness and focus the power of collaboration. I learned about *Evernote*, which is an incredible app that because of the way it syncs allows me to type up stuff, to take pictures, and to access material from any device with the downloaded app! So, while doing walkthroughs each day in the building, I walk around with my iPad and take notes using *Evernote* and then when I get home at night those notes are on my laptop. I learned about *Diigo*, an amazing tool whose potential I haven't even realized, which allows me to visit different websites, read through them, make notes or highlight parts of the text, and then bookmark it to my account so I can access it later. And that is just the beginning; other amazing tools include *mentimeter, yolasite, todaysmeet.com, typewith.me, twurdy,* and *socrative* just to name a few.

6. I shared the world of *Twitter* with my staff and colleagues through a voluntary training session which was attended by more than 40 people! It was great to see fellow educators get inspired and avail themselves of this new medium for professional development and for becoming a connected educator!

(Continued)

(Continued)

7. I started my own blog, which makes me feel empowered and allows me another outlet for my ideas, successes, failures, and passions as they relate to the world of education!

These are just a few of the things I learned since joining *Twitter* and sharing my tweets with the world. Needless to say, my professional development is now in my own hands and the experience is liberating! Sometimes I feel as if I am learning so much that I don't know where to begin, but I came up with a system for that, too—I use *Diigo*, a social bookmarking site to flag information that I want to hold on to and then I access it whenever I am ready to learn something new. I can honestly say that ever since I made the move from Isolation Island to the Island of Instructional Leaders not a day goes by where I don't learn something new!

Revitalizing the Staff Meeting

We live in a wonderfully tech-infused time, which means that we can change the original intent of a staff meeting: communication. These meetings herald from the age of pre-Internet, where most communication, no matter how minor, had to be delivered face-to-face. Mired in the old tradition of the principal as the main information giver, traditional staff meetings usually mean that participants sit-and-get information, then leave. In this fast-paced educational time, sit-and-get is no longer a great use of time, and yet many principals are not sure where to start in reclaiming these meetings. The staff meeting, with its built-in presence on the calendar, presents itself as a wonderful opportunity for a principal to signal a shift in power. It simply does not need to be a sit-and-get meeting anymore, but instead can be a marvelous opportunity for teachers to learn, collaborate, and innovate—all without having to find more time in their already busy schedules.

OBSTACLES

The biggest obstacle facing the staff meeting is the very history of the staff meeting itself. This old-fashioned meeting has created its own problems for years, and so you may find staff that are unwilling to believe it can be any different. However, through conversation and implementation, the staff meeting can be transformed into a powerful learning opportunity where staff feels empowered rather than exhausted.

BENEFITS OF CHANGE

By changing the very nature of the staff meeting, principals can expect

- a higher engagement whenever a meeting is called;
- a staff willing to share because they know their opinion is valued;
- an improved sense of community throughout the building;
- a sense of excitement for what is learned every day;
- a shared responsibility to make a meeting useful; and
- a sense of urgency for better time usage.

PLAN OF ACTION

Staff meetings' main purpose used to be information giving; how about making it information discussion instead? One way to get around all of the things that have to be regularly communicated is to send information as a school bulletin via e-mail. However, don't just send it out; set a clear expectation that staff should read it. Many e-mail services are equipped with a function that enables the sender to see if someone read the message. Set the expectation that e-mails are to be read, explain what the benefit is, and make it a part of official job responsibility. If some teachers choose not to read the e-mails, relay the information with a special meeting for them. Hopefully, they soon start to read instead of meet.

Rather than discuss upcoming professional development opportunities, make it a hands-on professional development opportunity. We tend to think of professional development (PD) as something secular, attended outside of school, and yet the staff meeting lends itself beautifully to a compressed staff development opportunity. With experts cultivated from within, staff meetings can become differentiated learning and discussion opportunities that leave staff with things to implement right now.

Don't just promise collaborative time, offer it right then. While many districts implement team meeting time into their schedules, many do not allow time for larger teams to meet. Staff meetings are perfect for having large teams meet to collaborate. Set the expectation that teams meet during this time, let them configure and plan their agenda beforehand, and then visit with the different groups. This is not to check up on teams, but rather to see where you, as the principal, are needed. Does anyone have a question only you can answer or a decision that needs to be made? Your role becomes one of visitor rather than leader.

No longer a principal responsibility, make the meeting a shared responsibility. The planning and leading of most staff meetings typically fall on the shoulders of the principal, yet teacher leaders are everywhere at a school, often waiting to be uncovered. Of course, the principals have much to add, but other staff members should be in charge of the agenda as well. However, do not expect people to just come out and take the responsibility; often, teachers need cajoling and direction before they become comfortable with the new format. Make it known that if the teachers want more out of staff meetings then they should be ready to bring something to the table to share, to discuss, to wonder about, or even to do. As a way to model the new format, lead by example and bring your own learning to share and remember to keep it short. If people don't naturally step up to take on the leading responsibilities, have different teams plan the meetings. This way every voice gets a turn.

Rather than closing off meetings to parents and students, sometimes invite their voices to the mix. Too often these stakeholders are left out of a school's professional discussion—it is time to change that. While certain topics do not invite outside participation, some do. Thus, by offering a platform for parents and students to share thoughts, you are starting a community discussion about what matters to everyone. Often we have hidden experts within our student and parent communities as well; it is time we tap into them.

Make the goal of the meeting to learn something useful, not just a discussion point. Frequently giving straight information is confused as learning something and while having more information is certainly helpful, often it is not something that can be implemented within classrooms the very next day. Why not make it a staff goal that after each meeting everyone leaves with at least one new thing they can use or try in their classrooms the very next day? Be explicit in the teaching, ask for input, and then allow time for others to share ideas. Make the staff meeting a hub of sharing rather than just a time for listening.

Rather than plan every minute, allow time for the extra things. Often all educators want is an extra 5 minutes to discuss something, try something, or share something. Often our tightly planned agendas do not allow this to happen. So, have the purpose of the meeting set, but leave 5 minutes at the beginning for staff to share ideas (note: preferably not at the end because meetings always seem to run late). Lead by example and highlight things you noticed in classroom observations or introduce your own ideas.

Trust your instincts for change. Every school's staff are distinct and function in their own ways. While my suggestions can be universally adopted, they do not cover every facet of change needed, so leave room for your own ideas for change as well, or even better, leave room for the ideas of those involved.

Peter DeWitt, an elementary school principal and author of the book *Flipping Leadership Doesn't Mean Reinventing the Wheel,* had another great idea—flipping the staff meeting. On the companion website you can see his ideas as well as suggestions on how to implement change in your school.

Cultivating the
Expert Within

The video started playing and hundreds of eyes focused in on a wonderful segment about teaching Shakespeare to elementary students and how we should never underestimate the abilities of our students to grasp and love complex materials. Yes, we were certainly inspired, but at the same time, most of us wondered why the outside video was shown. After all, we have our very own Shakespeare-loving teacher right in our district. Why didn't the video highlight her classroom rather than another teacher's work from the outside? Wasn't this the perfect opportunity to highlight an expert from within?

For years, districts have spent precious money bringing in experts from the outside. Whether hired as consultants to fix the achievement gap or to teach new strategies, serving as an expert is a profitable job in education. While many experts have earned that title and bring much value to a district, there is a path to professional development that should not be overlooked—using experts within the district—and it is cheaper. However, in many districts, inside experts are often overlooked, either through mere oversight, fear of creating jealousy, or because no one knows of their expertise. So, as a way to build confidence in our staff and save money in this budget-crunched era; it is time to cultivate the inside expert.

OBSTACLES

Fear of Standing Out

The most cited reason for why teachers do not advance their own expertise is for fear of standing out or the fear of people viewing it as self-aggrandizement. We may be the biggest cheerleaders when it comes to student success, but when success is within our own ranks, it is often met with jealousy, confusion, or even anger. While theories abound on why educators tear each other apart, it is a sad fact that often teachers are their own worst enemies. The ability to build a celebratory community successfully is best learned by example and should therefore be part of the goals set for the empowered school.

Lack of Knowledge

Sometimes districts do not tap into their inside experts because they have no idea that they exist. While this could just be an oversight, it can also be the sign of a bigger problem within the district, namely that there is no process to assess and record staff member assets and staff development. This is easily remedied by performing regular surveys of the staff.

Lack of Faith

Bringing in an outside expert appears to carry more authority than designating a teacher down the hall as the expert. Yet, often the outside experts began their careers as teachers down the hall who developed their own expertise into a new career. Therefore, it is important that districts encourage knowledge accrual by the teachers within their staff pool; it helps give confidence and support to their words. If a teacher is heralded as an expert, others start to agree, but someone must take that first step.

Narrowed Role

We tend to think of school staff as experts only within their grade level, or specialists only within one area. This shortsighted and narrow-minded view of professionals only damages and devalues the combined expertise within a district. While most staff are indeed experts on things that pertain to their immediate area of teaching, many staff are hidden experts in other areas; these people should be identified and their talents used.

BENEFITS OF CHANGE

By discovering and nurturing inside experts, districts gain

- a large pool of experts to pull from whenever needed;
- a more confident staff that believes it is okay to speak out about knowledge;
- a sharing, conducive environment where no idea is too minor to propose;
- a cheaper and more readily available solution to professional development; and
- a roster of inside experts that other districts can view and use as outside experts.

PLAN OF ACTION

First, ask people what they are good at. In one school where I worked, everyone could access a shared *Google* document where they were asked to reveal any special expertise which they could teach, not just within their academic areas. Our staff listed such diverse skills as website management, close reading instruction, and even lessons in juggling. This document was then shared and highlighted at a staff meeting. So, as a school, find a method to discover everyone's strengths using self-reflection, make the information easily accessible, and update it continually. That way, a database of expertise is started.

Second, discover the hidden experts. Ask your staff to describe the various proficiencies of their peers. In practice, certain people feel uncomfortable highlighting their talents, but may still be known as the go-to person of some skill. If you create a survey designed to define the expertise of others, it is easier to find their hidden talents.

Third, cultivate the expertise. Principals should automatically look to staff to lead sessions during staff meetings or during more structured professional development time. In fact, most staff development should be led by staff from within a district. Within a year, find as many opportunities as possible to truly cultivate your stable of experts and have them train others to become experts as well. This requires dedicating specific time for experts to teach and for people to learn. In the end, strive for everyone on the staff to become an expert in something.

Fourth, incorporate genius hour for teachers. If you are not familiar with genius hour, it is a practice used in classrooms around the world where students are given an hour to become experts on something. (For a further explanation, please visit our companion website.) Within my own classroom, I incorporate genius hour into science and social studies classes, allowing students free rein to explore and gather knowledge within certain topics. For teachers, this could be an hour-long exploration (perhaps in place of a staff meeting) where staff are asked to learn something new, either individually or through teams. Staff can then present their knowledge at a later date, but the emphasis should be on usability and expertise development. This approach is different from straight collaboration: rather than just figuring things out together, teachers are expected to learn something new.

Fifth, offer choice. Often in professional development, inquiries are deferred and teachers are told what they should study and learn. I did not become an expert on technology through time spent in my old district; however, I wish I had been given that opportunity. Therefore, allow teachers to pursue expertise in whichever area within education they choose. There is so much knowledge available, let teachers pick. It is important to have many different types of experts to support a larger knowledge acquisition for the school or district as a whole. When time and choice are given to staff, the buy-in is greater and so is the follow through.

Sixth, ask the staff. Along with offering choice, staff voice is vital for a successful transition. No more top-down decisions when it comes to staff development; instead, foster a genuine interest in what staff want to learn and where they want to develop expertise.

Finally, give it time. This small piece of advice crops up multiple times throughout this book. We cannot change our climate or culture overnight, but we can start on the path to change. So as much as it takes time to break bad habits, it also takes time to build new positive ones, and to secure buy-in to these changes. When called to participate as experts, certain team members may thrive right away and others may be reluctant. Find ways to make everyone comfortable and highlight the positive that everyone brings to the table. Becoming an expert is not just about acquiring knowledge; it is also about having the self-esteem to believe in one's own expertise. Confidence often comes from repeated interactions with others when they find value in what is shared; therefore, allow the time needed to have these interactions, whether big or small. Plant the seed of change, nurture it, reevaluate it every so often, and then watch the seed grow into a thriving plant. By the way, don't forget to share your own expertise.

Daisy Dyer Duerr, a principal at Saint Paul Schools, in Saint Paul, Arkansas, fully embraces the need for more empowered educators in her buildings. She shares the following advice to spread the power.

(Continued)

(Continued)

I am a PreK–12 principal. In fact, I am the only administrator on a four-building campus, and the only one within at least a 30-minute drive of my schools. Is teacher leadership important on my campus? To me, *important* is an understatement; CRUCIAL is what teacher leadership is to the success of our schools. Knowing that teacher leadership is so important, how do we as administrators make growing teacher leaders part of our focus? This conversion is not something that "just happens" overnight, or happens if you "will it." Building teacher leaders and nurturing a culture of teacher leadership takes work within your individual school community.

These are some of my core beliefs on building teacher leadership:

1. **Not All Teachers Are Leaders . . . and That's OK!**

This is very important to understand. Sometimes we want to mold people (including our students) into persons they are not. The opportunity to lead should be genuinely presented to our teachers; however, not all of them will be up for the task. Some of our really good teachers aren't leaders; that doesn't make them less effective or amazing as a classroom teacher, it just means they aren't a *teacher leader*. It's important to know the difference between teachers who may be reluctant leaders and teachers who are content with following teacher leaders. Knowing and appreciating the value of both is an important trait of an effective administrator.

2. **Ask a Lot . . . but Give a Lot in Return**

I ask my teachers to lead a LOT. For example during professional development days, my teachers are usually involved with at least 75 percent of the execution of these activities—and they perform flawlessly; they share best practices, administer hands-on activities, lead book studies, and communicate strategies with technology, just to name a few. How does this happen? I ask. I am an active participant in the training with the staff, and guess what—I learn a lot as well! Three years into my tenure at my school, cooperation like this is now part of the culture of our school. (I will not sugarcoat it and say it's been like this from the beginning; it hasn't.) Additionally, part of our culture involves me *giving* to my teachers. I've learned that the greatest gift I can give teachers is time. I work extremely hard to give my teachers extra planning times; I limit interruptions to instructional time; I let teachers leave early on days when it is important; and I cover teachers' duties virtually anytime they ask. *I center a huge portion of my leadership on trusting teachers' professionalism.*

3. Reluctant Leaders May Be Your Best Leaders

"Most people see leadership as a position and therefore don't see themselves as leaders."—Stephen R. Covey, American educator and author

I often hear teachers remark that taking a leadership role in school is a way of bragging or somehow saying that you are better than the other staff members. This attitude reminds me of what we deal with daily regarding the students in our schools. As an administrator, I persistently remind teachers that they have a "genius" that needs to be shared with the staff and this sharing ultimately helps the students; by being leaders in our schools, teachers are doing what's best for our students. I find that asking a teacher to show me something in a one on one or small group setting, they become more confident, thus more willing to share in a whole group setting. I have yet to encourage a teacher into taking a leadership role (where I supported them and helped them grow into this position) and not have him or her excel.

(Continued)

(Continued)

4. Commit to Building Leaders

"If your actions inspire others to dream more, learn more, do more and become more, you are a leader."—John Quincy Adams, 6th president of the United States

Let's face it; sometimes it's not easy getting people to lead. Teachers are no different when it comes to this maxim. There were times in the past when I was anxious and thought, "I'll just do this myself, it will be faster, easier, and I know I'll do a good job." If you get that feeling, ask yourself this question, "Will it be as effective if I do the job myself?" I always go back to this: leading in isolation is not effective— even for the best leaders. At the very least, great teacher leaders are the ones who get through to the teachers that you can't. (As principals there are always some people we can't reach.) As my high school geometry teacher always told me, "The sum is equal to the whole of its parts." I'm just one part of the whole at our school. I rely on my teacher leaders to bring all of our parts together to equal our sum.

I am proud to say that I am in a school where the culture is supportive of teacher leadership. If you don't have this culture in your school, take the time and work with your staff to develop it. It has really improved our school and made me proud to be a leader who shares leadership responsibility.

CHAPTER

4

Small Moment Professional Development

Professional development (PD) is a moneymaking business. Every day, schools and districts are bombarded with fancy catalogues, e-mails, and flyers that promise in the most efficient way possible the best professional development that money can buy. While many of these proposals are wonderful, in most districts there usually isn't the time or money available to secure such opportunities. Certainly at a school level, there isn't much opportunity for extensive professional development without asking staff to voluntarily attend. As a result, an event involving concentrated, outside experts brought in for professional development tends to happen only once or twice a year. For this reason, teachers start to think of professional development as something that only happens when it is marked on the calendar rather than as a positive growth opportunity that can regularly occur; it doesn't have to be this way. Professional development can happen and should happen every week, not through monopolizing huge blocks of teacher time, but through deliberately cultivating small moments to create learning opportunities. For example, establishing moments throughout the week where staff are encouraged to learn something new or to reach out to others for collaboration. Previously, we discussed the staff meeting as an opportunity for professional development; this chapter offers other suggestions on how to create these pockets of time for all staff.

OBSTACLES

Time

The biggest obstacle to weekly professional development will always be the element of time, which is why it is important to specifically define what counts as professional development. PD does not have to entail hour-long sessions or even involve large groups of people. PD can include 5 minutes of interaction, the length of an article or podcast, or even a 5-minute meeting. All of these small moments can add up to a lot of time, and that time accrues as true professional development.

Buy-In

Teachers are sometimes skeptical of new ideas, since teaching can often seem as a never-ending stream of new ideas. So, buy-in to a new idea can become a major point of contention with your staff. In the beginning, if possible make participation mandatory and give credit for the PD that is completed. Hopefully, as the year passes or participants become more involved, lay off the required mandatory attendance, but continue to give credit. While learning is always welcome, it is even better when credit is given for the training or for the shared benefits.

Ideas

Although I propose a list of ideas in the following plan of action section, remember that this is not a finite list. My hope is that as these ideas get rolling (and to keep PD in your school fresh and interesting), participants also come up with new ideas for small moment professional development.

BENEFITS OF CHANGE

By developing and implementing small moment professional development, schools can experience

- a more informed and enlightened staff;
- a staff ready to become inside experts;
- a greater informal collaboration;
- a joint passion for learning that trickles into classrooms;
- a better connected staff that is up-to-date with new initiatives; and
- a staff of experts who consult with other schools.

PLAN OF ACTION

The following plan of action to find small moments for PD is actually more of a list of ideas to get you started. However, the first suggestion is that you should not plan this list alone; a team approach (hopefully, a team that constantly adds new people to it) really benefits everyone. So, where can small moments of professional development happen?

- **Consider 5 minutes after the first bell.** This may be a sacred time for attendance, but why not dedicate it to reading time or video viewing time. Send a short blog post or article to your teachers to read during the first five minutes of the school day. Typically, students are settling in, working on morning work, listening to announcements, and getting ready for class to start. While you read, they can still be doing all those activities or they can also be reading a beneficial article. Another option is to have an article/video/podcast ready for staff in the morning—recognize that some teachers may wait until the first 5 minutes to review it while others may elect to do so earlier.

- **Create schoolwide independent reading time.** Once a day or once a week, the entire staff should drop everything and read. Often teachers think that independent reading time (if it is ever implemented) should be used to meet with students, grade papers, or prepare for class, but instead give permission to everyone to just read something. You can choose whether the reading material should be something predetermined or whether teachers can choose their own reading material, but give them the time.

- **Buy professional books for book clubs.** Some teachers thrive in informal book club discussions, but don't want to spend their own money buying the needed books. Therefore, why not allocate money for staff to pick their book club books and then highlight that there is a school book club. Often all it takes for teachers to start reading is to give them a nice, new inspiring book.

- **Forward on condensed and informative magazines.** One of the biggest obstacles to quick professional development is to find the time and topics to share. Magazines like *The Best and Next in Education* do the work for you. All you have to do is subscribe and then pass the issues on to staff.

- **Preload iPods with podcasts.** I know teachers who commute for more than 45 minutes to get to work, so why not have preloaded iPods ready for your staff to check out with great new podcasts? There are so many wonderful podcasts available for free that are designed to inspire teachers; many podcasts today are 10 to 15 minutes long, which means that even teachers driving short distances to school can benefit from this option. (To get inspired by the many listening choices, please see the companion website.)

- **Initiate the all-school read-in.** Why not use the gymnasium or cafeteria to have a weekly or biweekly read-in where teachers can drop their students off and meet in teams to learn something together? Frequently teachers are eager to learn, but they don't have the time to meet, so even a 30-minute read-in can provide the time with minimal supervision required.

- **Display articles in the bathroom.** The one place in the school that all teachers go at some point is the bathroom, so why not post relevant articles there? While this idea may seem silly or inappropriate to some, having reading material right in front of you usually means you will read it.

- **Bribe teachers with lunch or coffee.** Where there is food, there can be learning. Once a month, my incredible parent teacher organization (PTO) provides a teacher appreciation lunch, so why not combine this with a great video or discussion group meeting. While it cannot be made mandatory, if the content delivered is worthwhile, at least some teachers will choose to participate.

- **Combine PD with students.** Some of my best PD programs included conversations with my students after watching a video or reading an article. Now, these students were in the fifth grade so the content had to fit the appropriate age group, but I always left these student discussions with ideas to implement in our classroom the very next day.

Remember, this is not the ultimate catalogue, but rather a beginning list to spark ideas for you. Every school is different, as is its culture; brainstorm with both the teachers and students how to find the time for extra professional development. Create the opportunities and then showcase the teachers that take advantage of these circumstances. Direct them to leadership positions where they can share their newfound knowledge; after all, it is not just meant to provide teachers with more knowledge, but for them to become experts in their own right. Don't forget to be connected yourself. Whether that means tapped into a local network of leaders or a global association through *Twitter*, it is important to show the power of connection to your staff and to champion those who get connected.

Jay Posick, a principal in Merton, Wisconsin, has great success with implementing small moment PDs throughout his school. He writes

In Merton, we try to find ways to increase learning and collaboration time for our staff. This collaboration time can be focused on content or instructional practices and occurs

(Continued)

(Continued)

when staff have no supervisory or teaching responsibilities. Staff report to school 15 minutes early twice a month on Wednesdays for one of two different learning experiences.

1. One Wednesday a month, the principal takes the entire student body (about 500 students) into the gym for a 30-minute assembly from 8:45 to 9:15. This is an example of a presentation I have used. The learning and collaboration for staff begins at 8:00 and lasts until 9:15 (an hour and a half) and is driven by our school's Response to Intervention (RtI) team.

2. One Wednesday a month, we have a 30-minute meeting right before school in which staff have the opportunity to choose what they'd like to learn about, taught by members of our amazing staff. This learning is driven by our school's TILT (Teachers Integrating Learning Today) team.

We attempt to think out of the box when developing small moment professional development. In addition to our Wednesday morning meetings, we also held an EdCamp for an afternoon in which staff learned from one another while the superintendent and I chaperoned the students (about 500) in the gym. We hired a disc jockey (DJ), had board games in the commons, and some students asked to read in the library. This is something that was a surprise to our students and families, and somehow the staff kept it a secret. This learning was driven by our school's TILT team. We hosted *Twitter* Tuesdays to share the benefits of learning with *Twitter*. This year, we also had a voluntary book chat (*Teach Like a Pirate* by Dave Burgess) with staff who met before school. Additionally, we met one Monday evening to be involved in the #tlap *Twitter* chat where I provided pizza while we learned together. I also include tweets and blog posts in my weekly e-mail to staff.

The addition of these learning opportunities has been nothing short of wonderful. Staff do not need to miss class time for learning. With the exception of our RtI Wednesday, there is a great deal of staff choice in the learning. And, here's the best part: our own staff is leading the learning and learning from one another. That means we're learning from our own experts, and because they are our experts, they are a lot easier to contact for follow-up conversations and learning. As one of our teachers once said, "We are our best resource."

PART 2

The Need to Empower Our Teachers and Our Students

H is school file was the thickness of an elephant's trunk. In fact, it spanned so many referrals that it wasn't just one file, but many placed together in a larger file that was bursting. I only knew the child for two days and had my own impression, but now his file arrived to shatter that. That night as I read through reports from every single grade level and every year this child was in school and incidents covering minor disobedience to police involvement, my mind started spinning. How would this child fit into my vivacious classroom? How would this child react when I asked him to push himself further this year than ever before? When I asked him to do things that, according to his file, he would not be able to do? The only way to find out was to try, and so the next day I treated him as I did before I read the file, before the knowledge, and I asked him to do what every other child in the room was doing. So he did, and he tried and it wasn't perfect, but the day passed with no incident.

There are children that come into our classrooms bringing their reputation with them. They show up a couple of years before they become ours, their names carrying shudders and stories of recklessness and hatred of school. We see them coming for years and hope by the time they reach us that they have matured, that they have figured school out, or at the very least that they don't hate us as much as their other teachers. Then, there are the kids that are dropped into our classroom unannounced. They show up with a huge smile, perhaps even a hug for a strange new teacher, and within a day the honeymoon is over and their old nature comes out; in reality they are a destructive student, hell-bent on proving how awful school is. Call me crazy, but I love to teach those children; there is something about the power of their hatred for school that fuels my own desire to change the way school happens to these children. Those children are the ones that led me to creating an empowered student classroom because that is exactly what those children need—power. Once you give power to the hardest children you teach, handing it over to all of the other students becomes easy.

TEACHING STYLE REFLECTION

Empowered teachers know that to be a true changemaker, self-reflection is key. After all, one cannot exorcise any demons in an environment without knowing first which demons are caused by one's own mind-set or actions. Therefore, here are some questions to ask yourself as you begin this journey:

- Does my classroom trust me?
- Who typically decides how we learn something?
- What is my role in the classroom?
- How are students given a voice in the classroom?
- Who decides what needs to change in the classroom?

(Note: Visit our companion website where an in-depth form for self-reflection is provided.)

Once you complete this self-examination, now it is time to grow. Is there a specific area you want to conquer first, or if you are pretty happy with where you are as a teacher, perhaps only minor adjustments are needed? To set the tone for change, it is time to engage the students and declare your intentions.

DECLARATION OF INTENT

Now is the time to lay it out on the line, particularly if your decision to change is during a school year with your current group of students. We tend to hide our insecurities from students, and yet most students would trust us more if we showed more of our humanness. In the past when I worked on building community within a classroom, I always explain why this classroom may function a bit differently than what they are used to. I also discuss why I have a different classroom than what they may have encountered. I don't do it to gloat or to scare them, but rather to show why these changes are necessary for me to grow as a teacher and how these changes hopefully help them become more independent learners. Every year the discussion evolves and my reasoning and my expectations for the kids becomes more sophisticated. I no longer want them just to grow; I want them to thrive. So, I lay out my intentions and then ask them to join the conversation.

PLAN OF ACTION

Once the declaration has been made it is time to create a plan of action and vital to include student involvement. While you may decide to keep some changes private, this is really the time to discuss what the students would love to see change in the classroom. Of course, you may receive crazy ideas that can never be implemented, but within those ideas there should also be things that can. This process was how I discovered that my students would prefer to not face the Smartboard. I also discovered that they hated book talks with parents. The little things that students divulge can lead to more trust, particularly as you try to figure out how to change things that the students are suggesting. Lead a discussion on what matters within your classroom, what matters to these kids, and what they want to be a part of all the change. You may find that some students do not want anything to change; that is all right, just acknowledge that sentiment and move on. It is possible that no one offers any insight, therefore it is important to have questions to ask. A survey can help, or you may decide to have the students create the questions that they want to ask. You know your students best. The questions can be adapted to fit the changes that you want to see; if your main focus is to give students a voice to the world then questions can center on that intent. Another idea is to have a simple discussion with your class rather than a survey. It depends on how your class functions as a community, so select the format that can generate the most honest answers. While you may have your own ideas for how to start the discussion, here are some possible ideas to borrow.

Ask students

- What does the word "empowered" mean to you?
- What does an empowered student look like?
- What does not work for you in this classroom?
- What does it mean for students to have a voice?
- What is the one thing that this teacher must change?
- What is the one thing that has to change within our classroom?
- What is the one thing you hope we gain out of all of this?

As you progress in your plan of action, keep it simple. The process of empowering students should not be unmanageable or cumbersome, it should be something we can incorporate into already preexisting classroom structures by replacing some systems and traditions. Therefore, focus on what matters most to you and your students. Remember, you are trying to create an empowered classroom, consequently from now on you cannot be the only person making the big decisions. Of course, there will still be much for you to decide, but the students should feel a sense of shared responsibility when all is said and done. As everyone gets accustomed to the shift in power, more goals can be added to the plan. Again, I expect you will want to create goals that fit your specific classroom, but here are some goal examples:

- Students help plan lessons.
- Students connect globally via blogging.
- Students constructively criticize instruction and brainstorm better ways to learn.
- Students create their own learning opportunities.
- Students assess themselves and chart a path for their learning journey.

IMPLEMENTATION

Once classroom goals have been set, it is time to start. Pick one goal to work on and again turn to the students to ask for their ideas and then brainstorm how this goal can be reached. If a goal is to connect students globally, then decide on the medium to use to achieve this goal. Ways to connect globally are discussed in-depth on the companion website. Acknowledge that you also need to have a little faith at this point because even the savviest of students probably won't achieve success right away in a more student-owned environment.

As you embark on your journey to student empowerment, I hope you take a moment to reflect on all of the great things you already do in your room to benefit the students. Many teachers on the quest for change forget to celebrate all of the systems already in place in their classrooms—this is a shame since now is the time to congratulate yourself on what you have accomplished.

CHAPTER
5

The Empowered
Classroom

"I have an idea." The student marched over to me after I finished presenting their latest project. Up until now, this student had not said a word. She continued, "Is there a way that I could create a 3-D model based on the artist's life and present it to the class?" Since I wasn't sure what she meant, I asked for further explanation and what followed was a well-thought-out art project that more than fulfilled my requirements. My old self would have said no; after all, this was not what I envisioned as I planned my assessment. But, this version of me, the one pushing for student independence and learning driven by curiosity wanted to hoot and holler. This is exactly what the empowered student does; takes control of her own learning and makes it better. This student did exactly what I wanted, and she did it without my direction—I was so proud.

As you begin your journey to change, reflect on what you want to have in your power as a teacher? For example, power over my environment, actions, and decisions comes to mind for me. Our students are not much different. While they know that they have to go to school, they are more invested if they know that school includes them; that school is something they can also control. Therefore, in my vision there are four tenets to an empowered classroom: student voice, honest communication, sense of connection (knowing our place), and experimental learning. Although these tenets are discussed further in coming chapters, a brief overview is provided below.

Give students a voice—but also help them understand what it means to have a voice. Many of my students assume that having a voice just means speaking up, but to me it is much broader than that. Having a voice means having a say, a decision in what happens within the classroom or the school. Changing the way learning is provided and having a way to speak to the world. For information about amazing global projects and instruction and use of *Mystery Skype*, blogging, and *Twitter* in the classroom, please see our companion website.

Breed honesty. Frequently, our students are too nice to say how they really feel about school and what is happening to them, so it is imperative that educators lead by example with honest reflections and start discussions where students can safely share their true opinions and know that their words will not come back to haunt them in the future. Yes, honesty can hurt our pride as teachers, even mine, but I would rather know what I am doing wrong than have students pretend everything is okay.

Find your place. It is too simplistic to say that our place as teachers should be on the sidelines; it is also too simplistic to say that it should be as the leader. Instead, as a teacher our roles and our place changes every day and sometimes every minute. While one child may need you to hold their hand, another needs you to push them forward. One child may need you to get out of their way, while another is lost. I thought I would fail as a teacher if I led my students, now I know I only fail if I don't give them what they need.

Make room for failure and success. Too often we simplify failure and how we must embrace it because that is the only true way to learn. Yet, success is also needed. Sure students need perseverance, we all do, but we also need success to fuel our perseverance. If I set up a classroom where students continually failed, all in the name of creative pursuit, I would have a classroom full of students unsure that they would ever be able to succeed. Chance of failure—absolutely—but chance of success as well!

While empowering students is about more than simply this credo, this philosophy is the foundation that I use to build my classroom. These are the four tenets that must be in place for students to continue developing into incredibly passionate, confident, self-reliant problem solvers. Then, they can change the world, and not just when they grow up, but starting today.

OBSTACLES

Ourselves

We will always be our own worst enemies when it comes to implementing significant change in our classrooms. It is not that we don't think it is possible, we are just not certain that it is possible in our own classroom or that we are cut out for this type of learning. I know, I thought it too, and yet you just have to believe in yourself sometimes as much as you believe in your students.

Old Habits

As they say, old habits die hard, and in our classrooms this rings true. We are used to teaching in a way that follows a clear path to what we want students to know. Even if we don't lecture, and many teachers don't anymore, we are there to jump in whenever needed, constantly steering students in the right direction and making sure that they reach every small destination we mapped out for them. This old habit of managing students is hard to break, so the first step is to simply acknowledge it and allow yourself to back off a bit. After 4 years of change, I still have to remind myself that fifth grade is not about me, it is about the students in front of me.

Fear

Changing the way we teach can be terrifying. All of us are set in our ways, even if those ways regularly embrace change, but what am I am asking here can be a complete change in philosophy, and that can be frightening. So, you must have a little bit of faith, not in me, but in yourself and in your students. Most students will rise to the occasion and those are the ones to focus on first.

People's Perception

If you are the only teacher trying to empower your classroom, you may stick out like a sore thumb. Others may think you are crazy for trying to connect your students globally or having them complete lesson plans with you. It may help to get the administration on board by explaining your intent and your outcome; I have yet to meet a principal who does not want strong, self-driven, and motivated learners in their school. In the end, the best way to deal with a negative perception of you is to prove them wrong. Follow the path you chose and pour your dedication into it. Over the years, I have proven many people wrong, or rather my amazing students have.

Old Habits

Many of our students, even at the elementary level, think that school is something to just get through: they think they just need to show up, do what they are asked, and get through the day, the week, the year, until they finally graduate. School is a process with certain requirements and as long as those requirements are fulfilled then a child has done his part.

Confusion

At first, students may not understand what you are asking of them or why there needs to be a change in the classroom. In fact, some of my students always yearn for the "old ways" in the beginning of the year because the expectations were much clearer before. Expect confusion, do your best to support students through clear communication, and continue the discussion throughout the year.

Assumed Chaos

When I decided to hand power back to my students in ways that they learned and created, I assumed chaos would ensue. Students, after all, have been controlled by adults for so many years that I believed there was no way that my students would know what to do if I just let them loose. Those students proved me wrong, and I think yours will as well. So, acknowledge your own prejudices and assumptions about this way of teaching and try it anyway.

BENEFITS OF CHANGE

When I first started out changing the way control was distributed in our classroom, I was honest with my students. I told them I was sick of being the one always giving orders and that my 9-year-old self would have suffocated in our classroom environment. Not that I was doing anything wrong, it just wasn't an atmosphere that pushed students to become independent thinkers. My students must have thought it was a trick because they certainly were unsure how to respond. However, as I slowly proved to them that I was changing the way I taught and they learned, many amazing benefits started to evolve.

- **Joy.** What a simple yet powerful tool in learning. My students started to actually like coming to school.
- **Curiosity.** Whereas before my students asked what they needed to do to get something done, now they ask if they can go in different directions or take it further than expected. They are simply curious and want to know more.

- **Creativity**. I knew I had artists in our classroom, but I didn't know how many. My students repeatedly show me that there are many correct ways to learn something and to show off that learning.

- **Success**. Despite all of my previous best laid plans, I now have more success with students who disliked school than ever before. Often the students who need to be convinced that school is worthy of their time are the students that need school the most. Having students share control over the classroom gives power to some of the students who tend to have it the least. These students become more invested because it matters to them.

PLAN OF ACTION

Setting the tone for change most often starts with confronting your own teaching demons. What do you need to change and why? If you do not have a clear vision of what is standing in the way of the students' empowerment then it will be hard to move ahead with any kind of change. It is also important that you decide how much of a change is needed. Some people want to revamp their entire teaching style, while others would like to start with small steps or small changes. Wherever you fall in the range, evaluate and reflect on what matters to you and what you hope to gain from this change.

Whether you decide to share the power with your students at the beginning of the year, or on day 100, it is important to mark the change through discussion. I have always found that if I am forthcoming with what is going to happen, then students are much more willing to embrace and create the type of environment we desire. John Hattie stated it well in his 2009 book *Visible Learning:*

> Visible teaching and learning occurs when learning is the explicit goal, when it is appropriately challenging, when the teacher and student both (in their various ways) seek to ascertain whether and to what degree the challenging goal is

attained, when there is deliberate practice aimed at attaining mastery of the goal, when there is feedback given and sought, and when there are active, passionate, and engaging people (teacher, student, peers, and so on) participating in the act of learning. (p. 22)

It is therefore vital that student voice becomes part of your classroom, if it isn't already. Yet, to actively encourage students to take control of their learning journey requires a bit of work. Depending on your grade level, there can be years of ingrained "how to do school" habits to overcome. Therefore, this step should not be skipped or taken lightly because it is here where the foundation is prepared for what is to happen the rest of the year.

For better student understanding, I always lead the initial discussion with an eye on the end goal: students who feel like they are in control of their learning, fueled by curiosity, and eager to take on problems. In a similar manner to how teachers feel that they should have a voice in their schools, students should feel that they have a voice in their classroom. To borrow Hattie's words, he further states that visible learning

also refers to making teaching visible to the student, such that they learn to become their own teachers, which is the core attribute of lifelong learning or self-regulation, and of the love of learning that we so want students to value. (p.22)

Josh Stumpenhorst, a sixth-grade teacher in Naperville, Illinois leads the way for student empowerment in all schools through his own work. He writes

Allowing a student control over their learning should be a critical component of any classroom. For me, the simplest way to do this is through using the power of choice and student autonomy. When assigning projects or activities, I allow students various levels of choice. From what their final product will be to how they will gather information, I put the power in the student's hands. This not only serves as a powerful motivator, but empowers them to own their learning.

One specific thing we have done in our school to give ultimate power to students is through Genius Hour and Innovation Day. For Innovation Day we provide an entire school day every year for students to pursue learning they are passionate about. For example, if a student is interested in learning about stop-motion film, they spend their day learning how to create a film. Or, allowing the student who is interested in music to compose and perform his first guitar solo in front of his peers. The possibilities are endless when you give students control over what they learn and how they show their learning. In our school we took it a step further by introducing Genius Hour where students get one period a week to pursue learning of their choice. Similar to Innovation Day but on a weekly basis, students learn about topics of their choice and share their learning with their peers.

As schools, we have become very good at telling students what to learn, when to learn, how to learn and wonder why they are not motivated to learn. The more we empower students to control their own learning, the higher the motivation and therefore the higher the learning.

CHAPTER
6

Classroom Setup to Signal Change

While student voice is a term often coupled with the perspective and actions that students produce and bring forward into the world, when I use the term with my students it embraces a much larger meaning. I asked my students about student voice, and one of my students, Zach, responded with this explanation.

> I think that students should have a voice in a bunch of things, but most schools don't offer students a voice. I think that students should definitely have a voice in their grades. I think that if students can choose their grades, they won't get upset if they get a bad grade. Now, grades aren't the only thing that students should have an opinion in. I think that they

should have an opinion in how the classroom runs. I think that if the teacher makes up a bad rule the students should have every right to change it, because after all, they are the ones following the rules. I also think that the students should choose the assignments that they are given. Because what if the students don't prefer a style of assignment and then they get that type of assignment. Well, if students could choose what assignments they had, there wouldn't be a problem, would there?

Now, before anyone implements these changes, I recommend having a teacher have some opinion. Otherwise, kids might give themselves high grades even when they deserved a low one. So, I recommend if you do decide to implement student voice to have some way of reviewing the student's choice.

Now, I know that this might sound cheap and you might be thinking "Well, teachers have chosen grades, rules, and assignments for years," but honestly, no one likes to do stuff they don't like.

In the same way that we clamor for a voice in the decisions that affect us and feel outraged if no one listens, our students deserve a voice or a say in what happens to them. Most teachers, particularly at upper grades, already have some element of student voice incorporated, yet, it is easy to add more integration. However, student voice isn't just assimilated by the words that students say, but also where they say them, how they say them, and who listens to them. Student voice is even reflected by the very way our classrooms are structured. Therefore, after your student discussions, the very first place to start signaling change is within the setup of your classroom—the place where students express their voices.

The easiest way to signal shared control is through the very setup of your classroom. While some teachers still use the traditional desk setup where every student faces the teacher or the whiteboard, many teachers now realize that the classroom layout influences the type of learning that occurs. Hence, sharing power with students is symbolized in even the smallest things, such as access to supplies and where chairs are placed. This is also an easy thing to change for most teachers. Certainly, we all have our ways of how we like to work in the classroom, but physically moving things to promote more ownership is something that can be accomplished in little time with long-lasting effects. Usually, most teachers are stuck in the way they set up their rooms and find it hard to realistically find fault with the arrangement. Therefore, I suggest asking students for how well the classroom functions for them and to offer suggestions on how they might change it. I often find that I change my setup throughout the year to better suit the needs of the class, even if it just means little moves and not an entire classroom overhaul; remember that this should be a fluid process.

A simple learning environment where students can move about freely, where there is some room for different groups or for single person learning, and where the teacher is not all domineering is a classroom that signals shared power. A great place to start the change is through reflection: What does your classroom say about you?

OBSTACLES

I believe that the biggest obstacle to changing the design of our classrooms is because of our own lack of ideas. However, plenty of other obstacles can stand in our way and it becomes our mission to figure out how to work around them.

Lack of Funds

Most schools do not have unlimited funds and thus classroom furniture is not meant to inspire deep learning, but rather to last for many years to come. Due to fire codes, I invested very little money in my own classroom furniture, but found ways to work with the furniture I do have. So, rather than purchasing new items, use the pieces you have in a better way.

Lack of Space

Most grade-level classrooms are average size and normally must accommodate from 20 to 30+ students. As a result, I work with what I have; I get rid of unneeded furniture, and I am very selective about adding anything that takes away space.

Lack of Ideas

Frequently I am out of ideas on how to best make my classroom work, so I ask the students for their input. They never fail to come up with some new suggestions or some arrangement I had not considered.

BENEFITS OF CHANGE

If you walk into my classroom on any given day, you notice something right away; students are everywhere. This is not just because I have a large class, but because their workspaces are not contained to designated areas. Students sprawl out under tables, on the floor, on top of desks, in chairs, in corners, and wherever they feel the most comfortable. Students have various tools with them, whatever suits their needs, often flipping between computers and books and using whatever items they need to learn. Our furniture is moved as we see fit, and the students take care of our classroom with little prompting because they know that it is theirs to use. Since letting students design our space and change it as needed, many things have become apparent:

- More work gets done when students are comfortable.
- Students are better focused because they are not wiggling in place.
- Students think about what they need and simply get it.
- Students are more invested in what they are doing because they know they picked their spot and their setup.
- The classroom is cleaner because everyone assumes ownership.

PLAN OF ACTION

Classroom setup is personal and also something that can be outside of our control. Yet, there are many things you can consider as you move forward with your change. I added some questions to help you start.

- What is the overall feel of your classroom to newcomers?
- Is there room to move?
- What does the furniture setup signify—where does most furniture face?
- Is the furniture movable (whether physically or allowed by you)?
- Who owns the room?
- Do your things dominate the room or is there space for the students to carve out their space?
- If someone walks by your room, what do they notice?
- Are there different areas to spread into for different types of learners?
- How big is your desk? What vibe does your desk emit?

Once you reflect on your room setup and discuss it with the students, it is time to get to work. As elementary teachers, this task is made more difficult because, after all, our students are in the classrooms throughout most of the days. However, the challenge changes for middle and high school teachers since rooms often need to function for many students and lack space to spread out. This is the time where it is vital to be extra critical of what one needs while listening to the input of students. A great place to start is by eliminating unnecessary supplies and furniture, creating learning areas for students, and discussing with students how the room is a flexible learning space that can be changed to accommodate their needs. Little changes can include putting out supplies for students so that they do not need to ask you to borrow a pencil, eraser, stapler, and so forth. Remove or downsize your teacher desk to free up space and abolish the imposed barrier it creates between you and the students. You can also tell students that they can work anywhere in the room as long as they are productive and not bothering others. These three changes alone signal to students that this is also their room, not just yours, and that what happens within the room is something they can control.

As we progress through the school year, I continue to ask for student input. While the layout of the classroom starts with my setup, once the students are welcomed and we have worked for a few weeks, I ask them to take stock. What is working for us? What needs to change? Which areas are lacking in their room? Even the language used in these discussions is pertinent; this is "our" room not "my" room. They are asked to take responsibility for the room right away, and they are asked to cherish it as a learning environment, something which I model from day one. In fact, I asked this year's students what the perfect classroom looks like to them and Ella surprised me with her answer (edited for grammar):

> It's not supposed to be all the cool stuff you bought with your money, it's supposed to be about the environment! A classroom should look like a friendly, learning environment! A classroom with happy students and a happy teacher! The students should be taught enough information and taught well visually. Students should appreciate students' property and the teacher's property. Kids should be able to express themselves through their learning and their learning experiences. Students should get along well and help each other and solve out their problems themselves. The class should become a great big community!

We must strive for a great learning environment, but it will not exist if there isn't a great community being built as well. In the end, it is not the furniture we put into our classroom but the thought and care we place in it that helps build a community. Student empowerment does not just come from the physical features of the room, but also from the unspoken rules that govern us all; as teachers, the tone that we set from the very first day is vital.

Empowered Self—
Empowered Learning

"**B**ut, Mrs. Ripp, this is really boring." A student, in the middle of my meticulously planned grammar lesson, has just offered me his opinion, unsolicited and definitely not what I wanted to hear. It stopped me in my tracks and as I spun through retorts in my head ranging from "Well, what did you expect?" to "We just have to get through this," until I finally landed on, "Well, what can we do about it?" Although I didn't know it at the time, that was a landmark moment in my classroom. I don't remember how we ended up salvaging the lesson, but I remember the shocked response from my students as I asked them to take responsibility and help me create a better lesson, something they eagerly did. I knew after that lesson that I was onto something; so for the past four years, students have helped me plan many lessons. In fact, I recently wrote a blog post detailing that process, which greatly assists me as a teacher any time, but specifically now due to the early arrival of my fourth child, Augustine.

" . . . So what do you want to do?"

Five hands shoot into the air and our discussion quickly gets underway. As one student shares an idea for a long-term project, another quickly jumps in with their opinion, and a picture starts to emerge of just what we can accomplish. As students figure out whether they want to work alone or with partners, what they want to create, and the objective of the assignment, my brain begins to calm down. I knew the students would know what to do; I knew the students would have a better idea than mine. And now, after 15 minutes of discussion, the organization plan for socials studies for the next four weeks is prepared with every student excited and aware of his or her role. Welcome to lesson planning in my classroom.

Augustine didn't care that I had not written substitute plans; nor did she care that we had no substitute. She arrived when she wanted and I have furiously been trying to keep my classroom "normal" ever since that day. Or, at least as normal as you can when you have different subs every day and your brain is muddled with medical terms you never knew before. This week I returned to school part-time, not just to offer my students a sense of transition to a long-term sub, but also to see if they were up for the biggest challenge of the year—working independently with teachers as coaches, not leaders. And oh, are they ever.

All year, I push my students to be independent learners, to carve their own path, to take control of how they learn something, not just how much they learn. All year, I challenge them to speak up, to step up, and to push for a better education. An education that revolves more around their own needs rather than just what the curriculum dictates. I tell them they need to be independent learners; I push them to become independent learners. Now is their time to actually practice it.

(Continued)

(Continued)

We don't know who the substitutes will be, we hope they will come back more than once, but we have to plan as if every afternoon brings a new face with no concept of our procedures. So, the students and I decided that together we would devise a plan that covered all of the curriculum, but freed up a poor sub from reading lengthy lesson plans, and my students from being taught straight out of the book.

I could have insisted on my own project. I could have told them the exact plan. I could have created a great learning opportunity for them. But, I needed their buy-in; I needed their excitement and their independence for this to work. As a result, instead of more me, it became more them. Instead of more text book, it became more research. Instead of one size fits all, we now have more than 20 student-driven projects ready to present to any substitute. All of the students will learn the material; all of them will become experts on something; all of them will create; and all of them had something to say.

When was the last time you let your students construct the lesson plan with you?

Even though students don't plan every lesson with me, there is always an element of student voice within our lessons. Often, I tell students the end goal of the lesson and then they figure out ways to get there. We try to leave it open for many interpretations and ideas so that students become invested in the learning, not because I asked them to, but because they want to. As a teacher, this type of personalized learning also means that no year is ever the same; new students mean new ideas; and I grow as a learner right along with my students as I continue to hone the process of pushing students to achieve, and more importantly, to reignite their curiosity.

Personalized learning and student ownership go hand in hand, but the transition can seem daunting to many teachers. Before you create your plan of action, remember that many obstacles are simply perceptions to overcome before we can fully invest ourselves, so take the time you need to think through these obstacles and how they affect you as a teacher.

OBSTACLES

Teacher as Controller

As the only adult in the classroom, the assumption is that we must always stay in control and that student-owned learning means that we are relinquishing that control. However, that is not the case; as teachers we are not transferring complete ownership of the classroom, but instead shifting the balance of control to include the students.

Assumed Chaos

Once a power structure has shifted, we falsely assume that students will take full advantage of the situation and that chaos will reign supreme. However, in my experience I can assure you that this is not the case; instead, when students are given control over their learning, working with a teacher who knows their goal direction, they are more invested, more focused, and generally speaking better students. This is a process and there will be growing pains, but chaos should not be a part of that.

Predetermined Lesson Plans

In some school districts there are predetermined lesson plans that impede any kind of personalization. While I work within district controlled curriculum, I always find a way to include student changes. Even communicating to students that there are choices to be made by them, however minor, can be a powerful buy-in generator. Sometimes a change as small as where they work or who they work with can be enough to increase student engagement, so remember that student empowerment can come in many shapes and sizes.

Time

Often lesson planning is done after the students leave and when teachers can finally find a moment to breathe; shifting this task into actual classroom time can be seen as wasteful. However, the time I spend lesson planning with my students often comes from the time I use to explain the next assignment, or define the project, or teach a segment. In the long run, using a student-owned approach, we are able to fit as much, if not more, learning into our curriculum calendar.

BENEFITS OF CHANGE

The biggest benefit of empowered learning is student empowerment, but other advantages include

- increased understanding of curriculum;
- amplified development of independent learners and problem solvers;
- absence of stagnant units taught the same way year after year;
- increased student enthusiasm and engagement; and
- improved community since students have a voice.

PLAN OF ACTION

While there are many ways to start the process of handing over power to students, I detailed my own path to show you an example. Again, make the process work for you and your students. Since you already included students in lesson plan development and began to show them what an empowered classroom looks and feels like, draw on their ideas as you start the process.

Questions to ask yourself before you plan:

- What is it that students brought up that they wanted from school and how can that be incorporated into your lessons?

- What are the dynamics of the class, how old are the students, are they adventurers or more conservative?
- How do they function when working together?
- How much independence are they used to?

In my experience, students need a bit of support to start adding their voice to the lessons. Ask your class for their craziest ideas and then work backwards. You can start small and simply have students plan the final product or you can suggest they plan everything: product, process, and assessment. There is no wrong way to start.

This also marks the beginning of a journey for your students. They are starting their path to becoming more demanding consumers of learning, and this requires that they take the time to reflect on what their strengths and weaknesses are, as well as what they hope to gain out of their education. I created a sample student reflection form that is posted on our companion website. In the end, the hope is that students start to direct their own learning, honed by their curiosity, and propelled further by their eagerness to learn. This does not happen overnight and requires work both from the teacher and from the students; particularly as you start out, be sure to dedicate time to this transition. Treat this process as an important investment in the rest of the school year. Once you plan your first lesson together, make certain to take time at the end of the lesson to reflect and review. This is particularly important for students as they get used to taking ownership of what they learned rather than just being told how they did in a unit or project. My students complete this reflection and review using many methods: classroom discussions with me as a notetaker, through surveys, or even informally on quick post-it notes. The intensity of the reflection depends on the size of the project, as well as the investment of the students. If a project does not go as planned, always take the time to have a deeper conversation about what went wrong.

As the final component, I encourage teachers to have students perform a self-assessment, either in conjunction with a teacher assessment or alone. Often a student's assessment reveals areas for improvement that I might not notice, or students share thoughts on how they choose to progress. In my classroom assessment, this evaluation is essential since it is not for a grade (I don't use grades except for trimester report cards), but rather is for setting new goals in their learning journey. When students assess themselves and each other, they quickly discover what they still need to work on, and then start to come up with ways that they can reach these goals. By taking control over their assessment, students naturally feel in control of their performance. They know how they are assessed and what they need to do to improve. In my eyes, this knowledge is more powerful than any grade will ever be.

Conclusion

S imilar to the child who is given no power over his or her day, educators who have limited power in their school environments slowly lose their dedication and passion for school. It takes extra effort to get excited or engaged in the presented material, and slowly opportunities that could otherwise recharge us are instead viewed as just more work. Our students experience the same lack of excitement as we slowly remove all control from them by teaching them to conform and to simply sit still and listen. Yet, we forget that schools should be joyful, that classrooms should be venues for exploration, and that communities should be built around shared responsibility and shared power. As a leader, because we are all leaders in some capacity, you can decide whether to create an environment that promotes growth, or one that promotes compliance.

Every day we make a choice. As leaders within our schools or within our classrooms, we choose whether to empower or to take away control. We choose whether to teach others how to lead and make room for independence, or we choose to continually and blindly follow whatever directions have been set. It is a choice we make, whether consciously or not, and it directly affects the lives and passions of others. As teachers we hold that immense power within us every day, in every moment, and yet we often forget what our decisions mean for others. This is why empowering schools and students is instrumental to future success. This is why change doesn't have to be big to be meaningful; it can start small with one decision that then leads to another and another. Change doesn't have to be dramatic, it doesn't have to be painful; it can be easy, it can be minor, and yet it can still carry great power.

I never meant to empower my students, not in the beginning anyway. I just wanted a classroom where students felt that they had a say, where they felt in control, not just of themselves, but of their journey as learners. Now, looking back on my own journey within the connected educator community, I see that it was not just my students who needed a place to find their voice, I needed to find my own voice as well. Becoming an empowered connected educator has done just that for me. It provides me with a way to show the world how education can be done if we trust our students and ourselves. If we trust those around us to make great decisions, if we encourage open dialogue within our school communities, and if we involve all stakeholders and not just those that we deem most important, great things can happen.

In the end, an empowered school or classroom is a space where everyone has a place. Where everyone feels heard, respected, and believes they can make a difference. Where follow-through and passionate leadership from many sources are celebrated. Where new ideas are discussed in the open with consideration given to all sides. Where everyone has a voice. It is not too late to change; you have taken the first step today.

A SAGE Company

Corwin is committed to improving education for all learners by publishing books and other professional development resources for those serving the field of PreK–12 education. By providing practical, hands-on materials, Corwin continues to carry out the promise of its motto: **"Helping Educators Do Their Work Better."**